Planned by Joanne Wylie
Illustrated by Bunky.

**grades 2 and 3**

# multiply and divide

practice in multiplying and dividing
numbers from one to ten

A WHITMAN BOOK
Western Publishing Company, Inc.
Racine, Wisconsin

# ×××× multiplication ××××

Count the number of objects in each set.
Write that number in the top box.
That is one <u>factor</u>.

How many sets are there?
That number is in the middle box.
That is the other <u>factor</u>.

Count the number of objects when
the sets are joined.
Write that number in the bottom box.
That is the <u>product</u>.

<u>Multiplication</u> is naming the missing product.

2

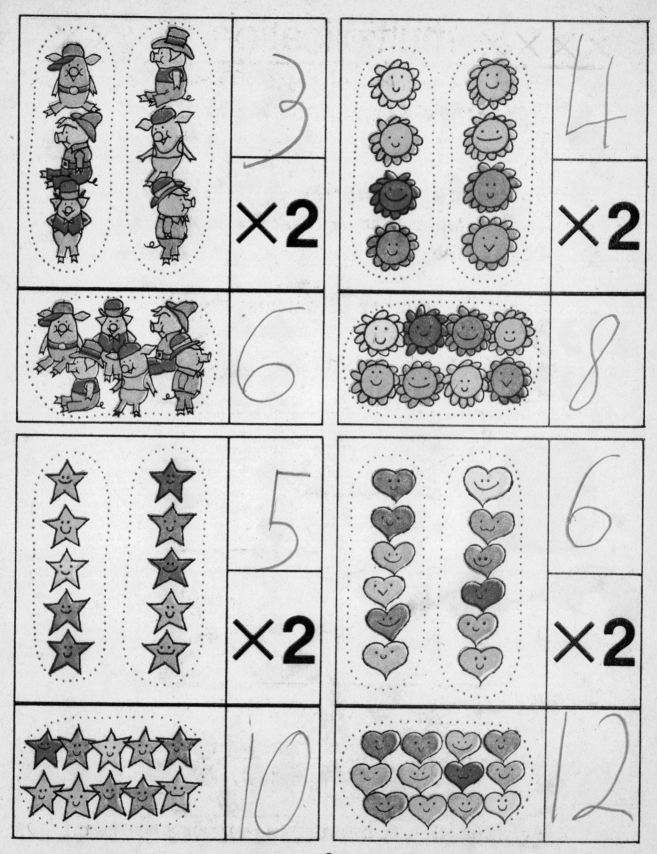

3

7

×2

14

8

×2

16

9

×2

18

4

**Starting from zero, jump to the right. You will see that multiplying is a short way of adding the same number again and again. Put your answer in the box at the right.**

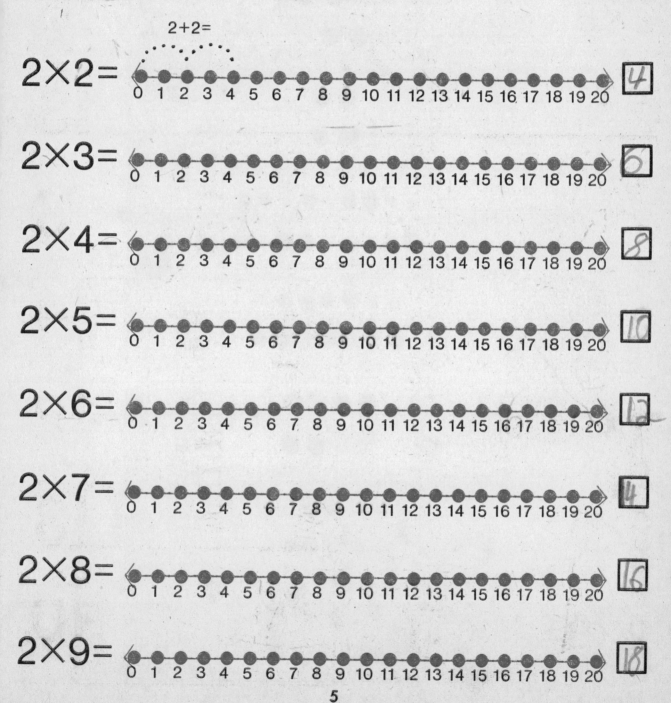

2×2= 4

2×3= 6

2×4= 8

2×5= 10

2×6= 12

2×7= 4

2×8= 16

2×9= 18

$2\times2=$

$2\times8=$

$2\times4=$

$2\times7=$

$2\times3=$

$2\times9=$

$2\times5=$

$2\times6=$

14

6

16

8

4

12

18

10

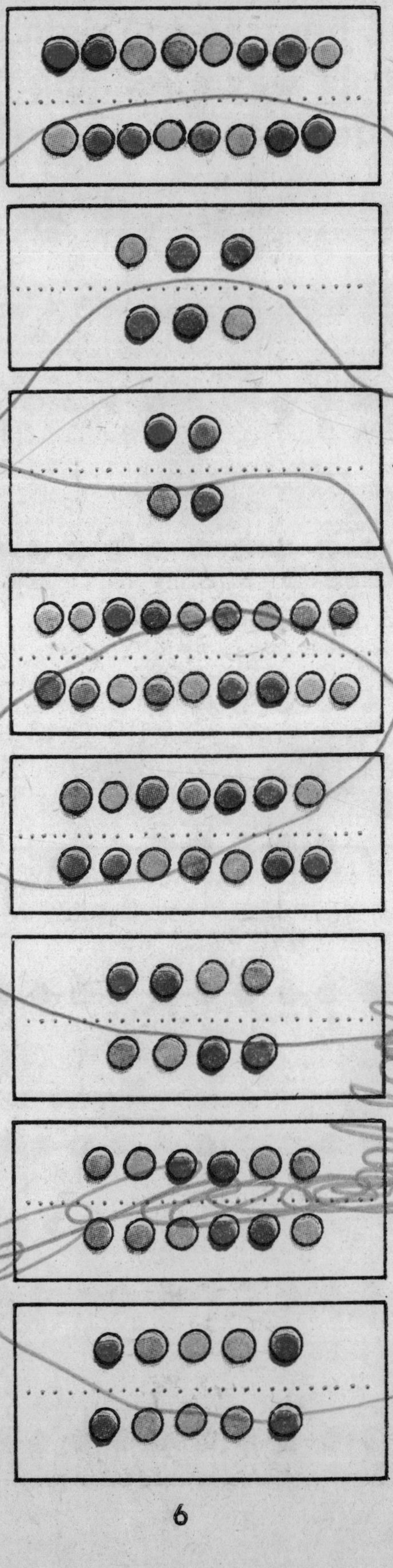

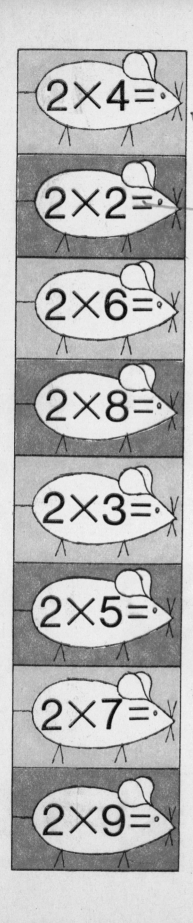

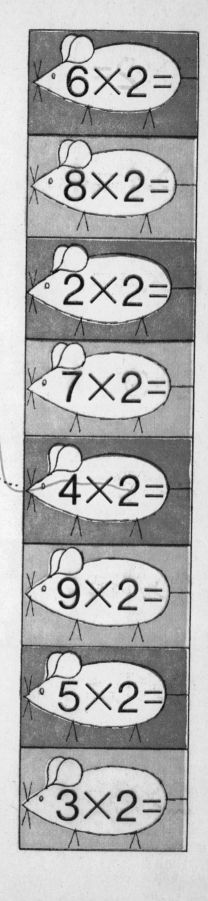

2×4=

2×2=

2×6=

2×8=

2×3=

2×5=

2×7=

2×9=

12

4

6

8

14

16

18

10

6×2=

8×2=

2×2=

7×2=

4×2=

9×2=

5×2=

3×2=

7

# Draw a line to connect the two factors
## that make the product when one factor is 2.

2×2

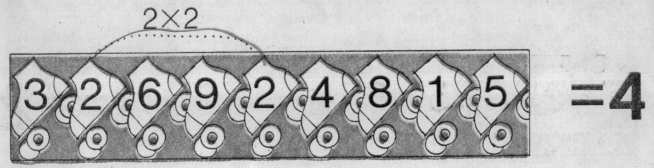

3 2 6 9 2 4 8 1 5 **=4**

2 8 5 7 3 1 6 9 4 **=6**

1 5 2 9 4 6 8 3 7 **=8**

6 3 7 2 9 5 4 1 8 **=10**

7 2 3 5 6 8 4 9 1 =12

3 2 1 7 4 9 5 8 6 =14

9 1 2 3 4 5 8 6 7 =16

5 3 7 2 9 4 1 6 8 =18

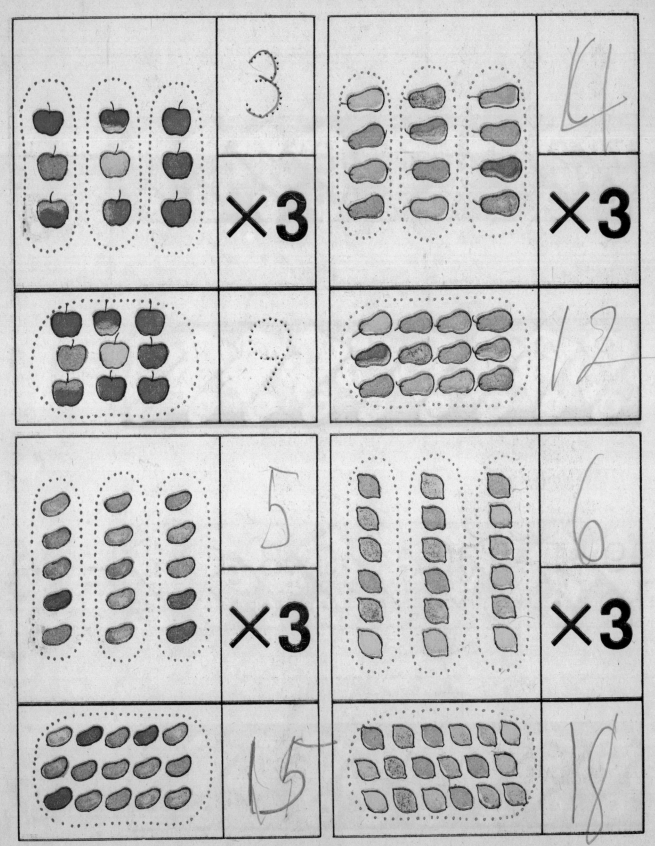

3
×3

9

4
×3

12

5
×3

15

6
×3

18

10

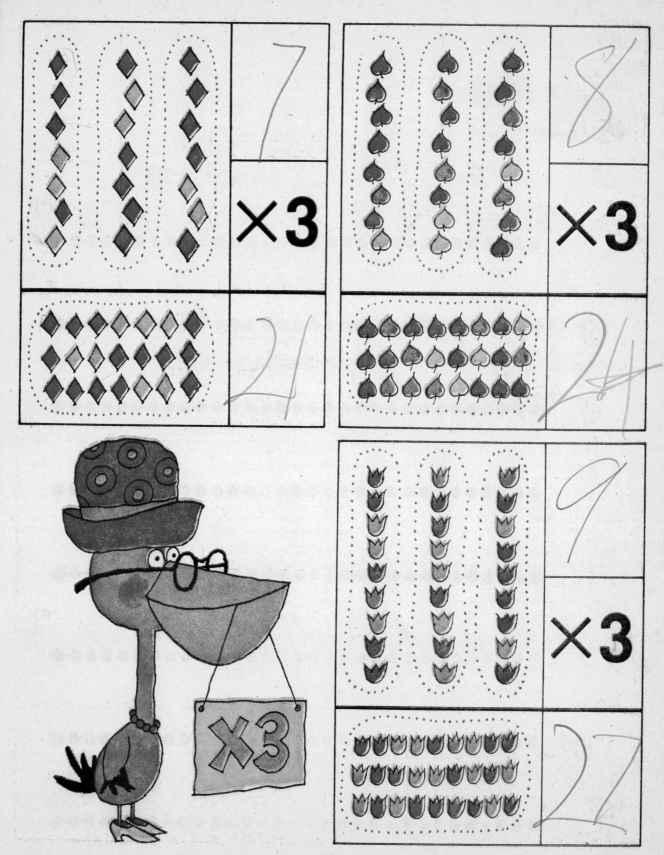

7
×3
21

8
×3
24

9
×3
27

×3

11

**Starting from zero, jump to the right. Put your answer in the box at the right.**

2+2+2=

$3 \times 2 =$ 0 1 2 3 4 5 6 7 8 9 10 11 12 13 14 15 16 17 18 19 20 21 22 23 24 25 26 27 28 29 30

$3 \times 3 =$ 0 1 2 3 4 5 6 7 8 9 10 11 12 13 14 15 16 17 18 19 20 21 22 23 24 25 26 27 28 29 30 [9]

$3 \times 4 =$ 0 1 2 3 4 5 6 7 8 9 10 11 12 13 14 15 16 17 18 19 20 21 22 23 24 25 26 27 28 29 30

$3 \times 5 =$ 0 1 2 3 4 5 6 7 8 9 10 11 12 13 14 15 16 17 18 19 20 21 22 23 24 25 26 27 28 29 30

$3 \times 6 =$ 0 1 2 3 4 5 6 7 8 9 10 11 12 13 14 15 16 17 18 19 20 21 22 23 24 25 26 27 28 29 30

$3 \times 7 =$ 0 1 2 3 4 5 6 7 8 9 10 11 12 13 14 15 16 17 18 19 20 21 22 23 24 25 26 27 28 29 30

$3 \times 8 =$ 0 1 2 3 4 5 6 7 8 9 10 11 12 13 14 15 16 17 18 19 20 21 22 23 24 25 26 27 28 29 30

$3 \times 9 =$ 0 1 2 3 4 5 6 7 8 9 10 11 12 13 14 15 16 17 18 19 20 21 22 23 24 25 26 27 28 29 30

$3 \times 3 =$

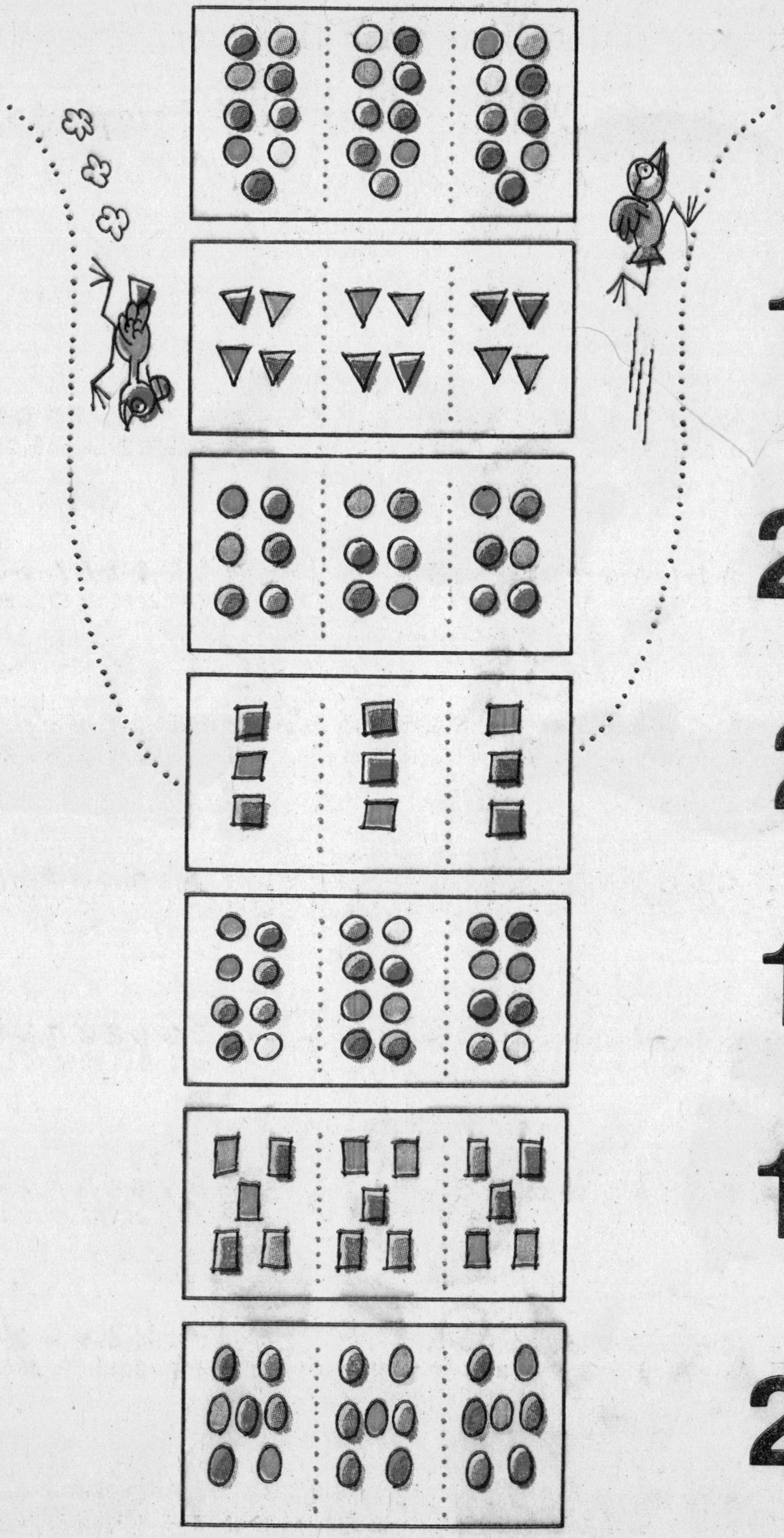

$3 \times 6 =$

$3 \times 9 =$

$3 \times 4 =$

$3 \times 5 =$

$3 \times 7 =$

$3 \times 8 =$

**9**

**15**

**27**

**21**

**18**

**12**

**24**

# Circle the animal with the correct product number on its shirt.

3×6=    12    18

3×9=    27    24

3×3=    6    9

3×5=    12    15

15

$3 \times 5 =$

$3 \times 9 =$

$3 \times 3 =$

$3 \times 6 =$

$3 \times 4 =$

$3 \times 8 =$

$3 \times 7 =$

18

24

27

15

9

21

12

$9 \times 3 =$

$3 \times 3 =$

$8 \times 3 =$

$6 \times 3 =$

$7 \times 3 =$

$5 \times 3 =$

$4 \times 3 =$

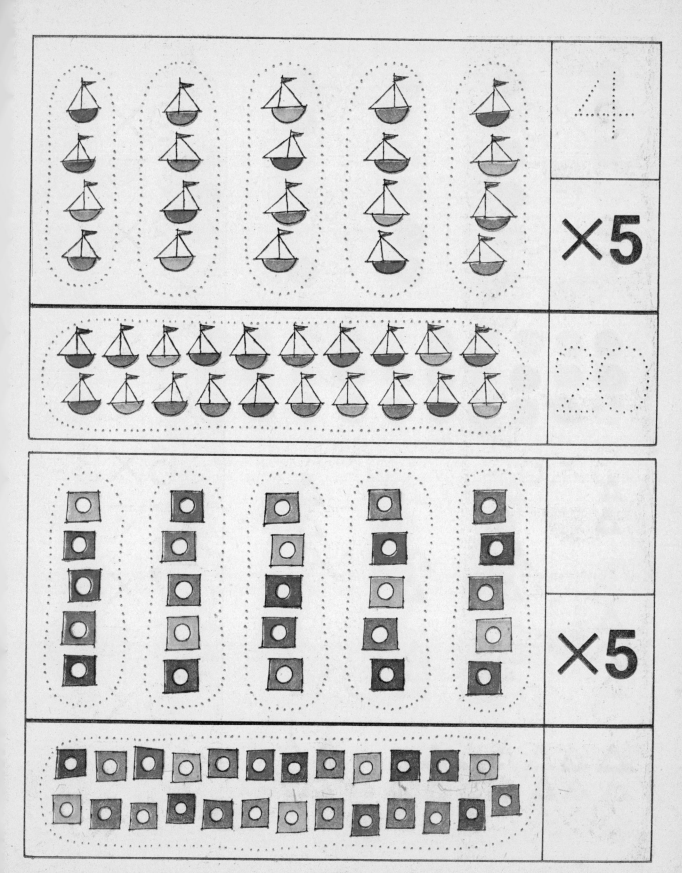

4

×5

20

×5

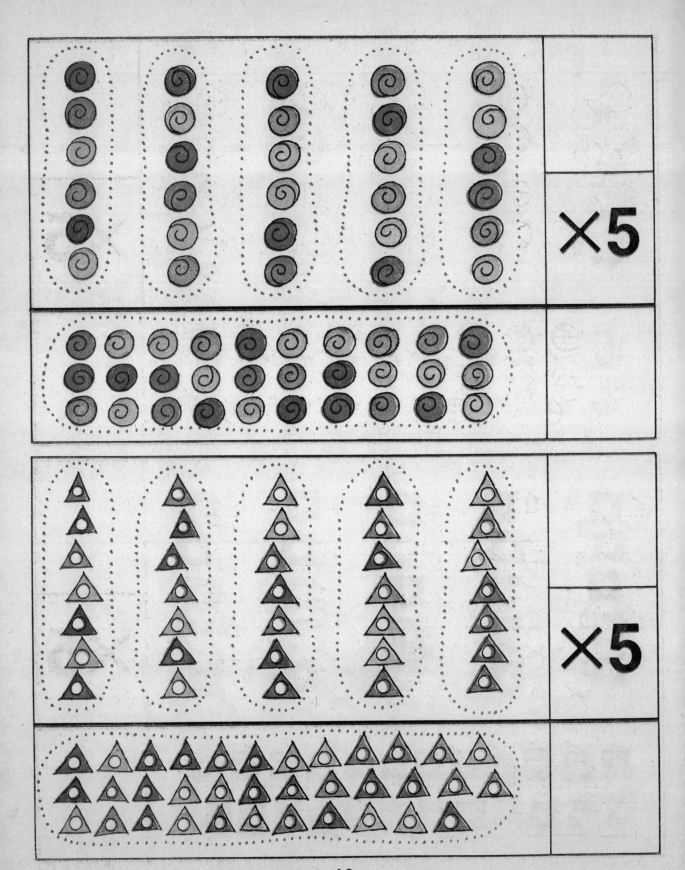

×5

×5

18

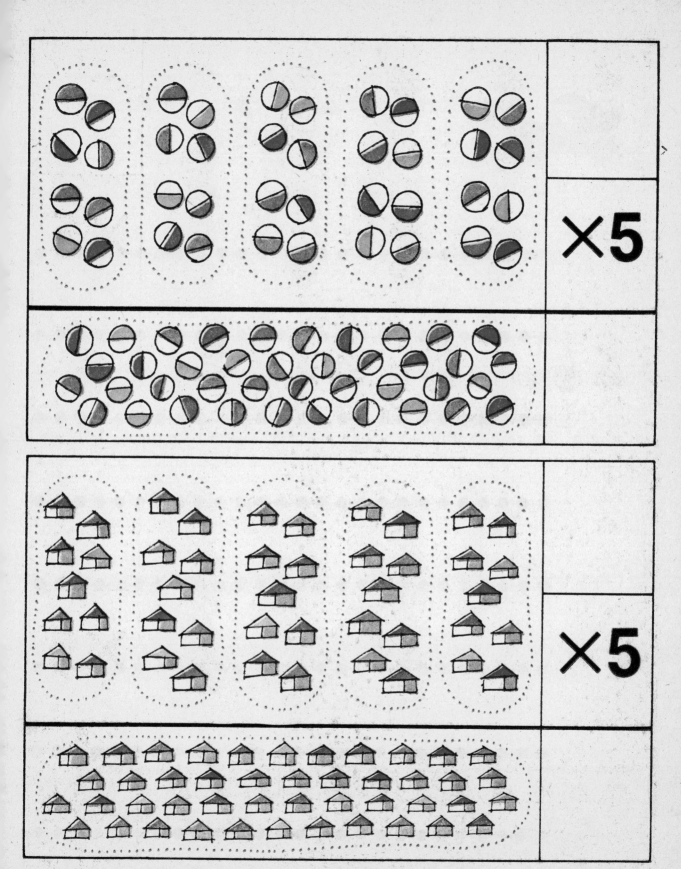

**Starting from zero, jump to the right.**
**Put your answer in the box at the right.**

$2 + 2 + 2 + 2 + 2 =$

$5 \times 2 =$
0 1 2 3 4 5 6 7 8 9 10 11 12 13 14 15 16 17 18 19 20 21 22 23 24 25

$5 \times 3 =$
0 1 2 3 4 5 6 7 8 9 10 11 12 13 14 15 16 17 18 19 20 21 22 23 24 25

$5 \times 4 =$
0 1 2 3 4 5 6 7 8 9 10 11 12 13 14 15 16 17 18 19 20 21 22 23 24 25

$5 \times 5 =$
0 1 2 3 4 5 6 7 8 9 10 11 12 13 14 15 16 17 18 19 20 21 22 23 24 25

$5 \times 6 =$
0 1 2 3 4 5 6 7 8 9 10 11 12 13 14 15 16 17 18 19 20 21 22 23 24 25

$5 \times 7 =$
0 1 2 3 4 5 6 7 8 9 10 11 12 13 14 15 16 17 18 19 20 21 22 23 24 25

$5 \times 8 =$
0 1 2 3 4 5 6 7 8 9 10 11 12 13 14 15 16 17 18 19 20 21 22 23 24 25

$5 \times 9 =$
0 1 2 3 4 5 6 7 8 9 10 11 12 13 14 15 16 17 18 19 20 21 22 23 24 25

26 27 28 29 30 31 32 33 34 35 36 37 38 39 40 41 42 43 44 45 46 47 48 49 50

26 27 28 29 30 31 32 33 34 35 36 37 38 39 40 41 42 43 44 45 46 47 48 49 50

26 27 28 29 30 31 32 33 34 35 36 37 38 39 40 41 42 43 44 45 46 47 48 49 50

26 27 28 29 30 31 32 33 34 35 36 37 38 39 40 41 42 43 44 45 46 47 48 49 50

26 27 28 29 30 31 32 33 34 35 36 37 38 39 40 41 42 43 44 45 46 47 48 49 50

26 27 28 29 30 31 32 33 34 35 36 37 38 39 40 41 42 43 44 45 46 47 48 49 50

26 27 28 29 30 31 32 33 34 35 36 37 38 39 40 41 42 43 44 45 46 47 48 49 50

26 27 28 29 30 31 32 33 34 35 36 37 38 39 40 41 42 43 44 45 46 47 48 49 50

$5 \times 6 =$      **25**

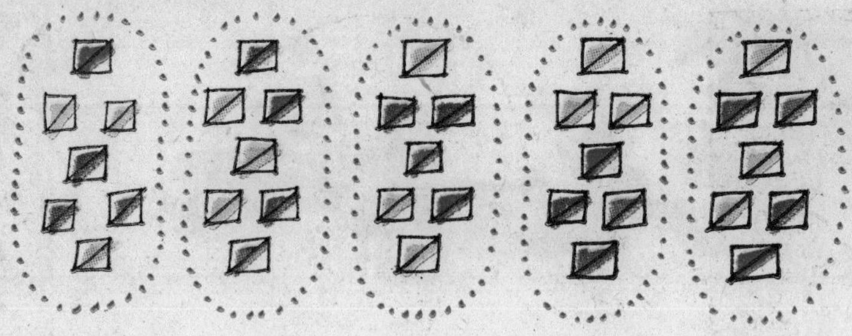

$5 \times 4 =$      **35**

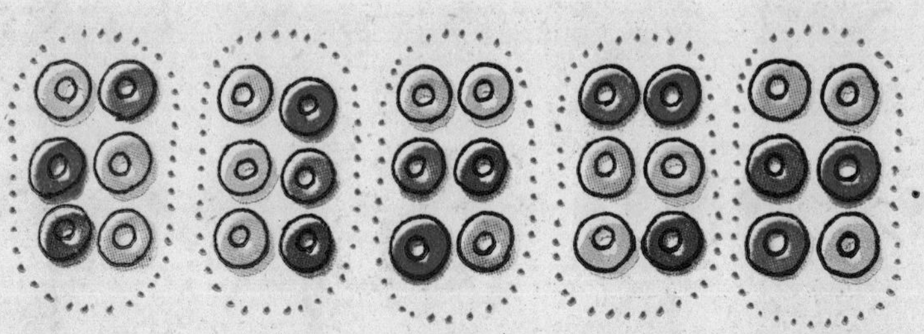

$5 \times 5 =$      **40**

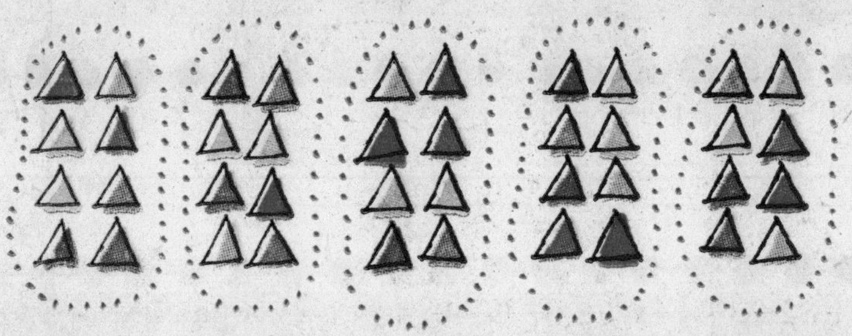

$5 \times 8 =$      **45**

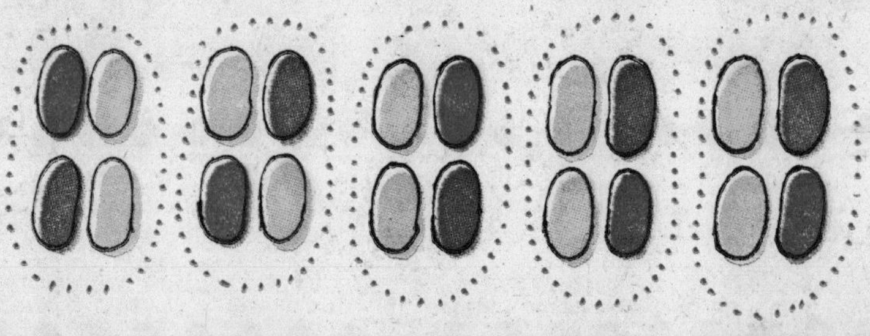

$5 \times 7 =$      **30**

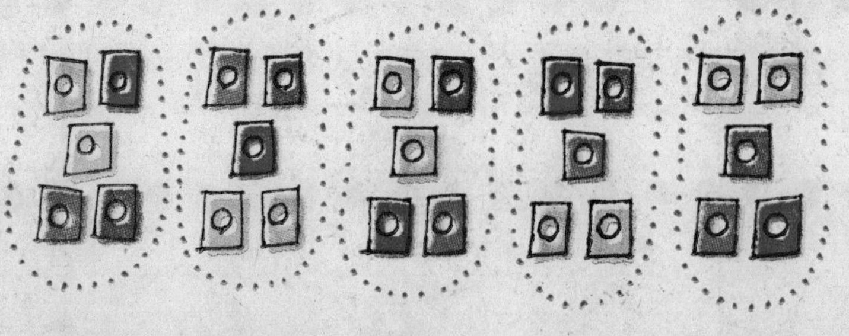

$5 \times 9 =$      **20**

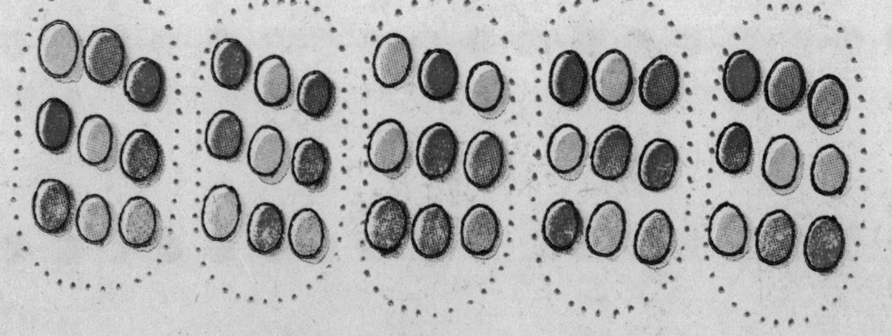

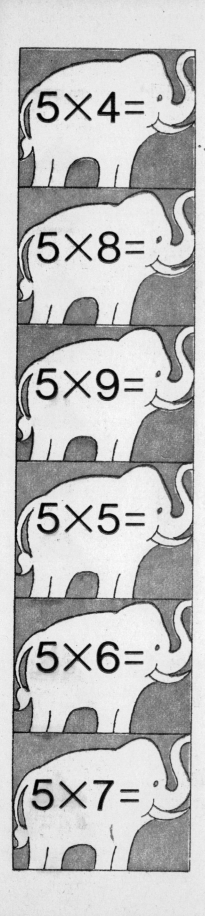

5×4=

5×8=

5×9=

5×5=

5×6=

5×7=

25

20

35

40

30

45

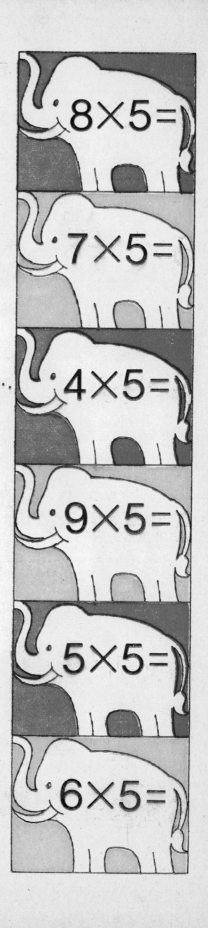

8×5=

7×5=

4×5=

9×5=

5×5=

6×5=

**Draw a line from each fire fighter's hose to the fire hydrant with the missing product number.**

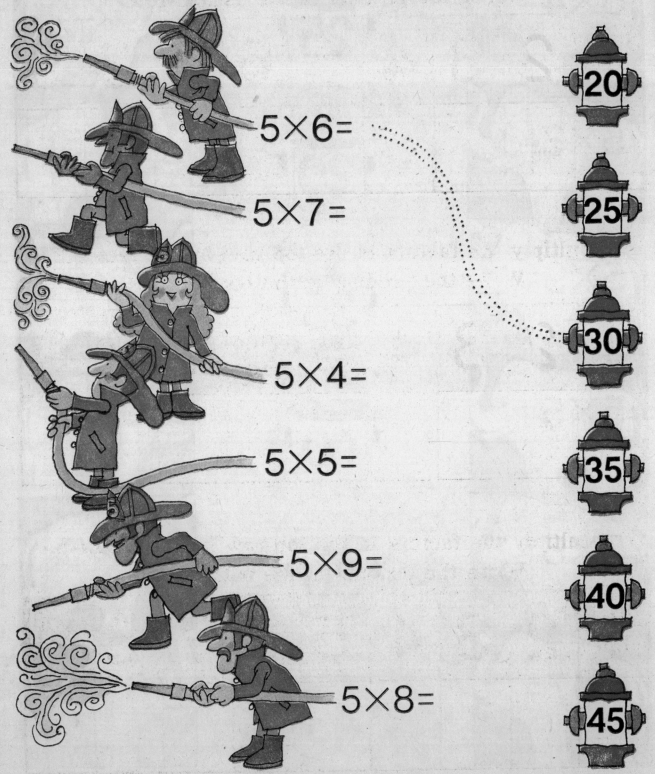

$5\times6=$

$5\times7=$

$5\times4=$

$5\times5=$

$5\times9=$

$5\times8=$

20

25

30

35

40

45

**Multiply the factors in the top row by the factor 2.**
**Write the product in the bottom row.**

| 1 | 2 | 3 | 4 | 5 | 6 | 7 | 8 | 9 |
|---|---|---|---|---|---|---|---|---|
|   | 4 |   |   |   |   |   |   |   |

**Multiply the factors in the top row by the factor 3.**
**Write the product in the bottom row.**

| 1 | 2 | 3 | 4 | 5 | 6 | 7 | 8 | 9 |
|---|---|---|---|---|---|---|---|---|
|   | 6 |   |   |   |   |   |   |   |

**Multiply the factors in the top row by the factor 5.**
**Write the product in the bottom row.**

| 1 | 2 | 3 | 4 | 5 | 6 | 7 | 8 | 9 |
|---|---|---|---|---|---|---|---|---|
|   | 10 |   |   |   |   |   |   |   |

$2 \times 2 =$ ☐
$3 \times 3 =$ ☐
$5 \times 5 =$ ☐
$2 \times 3 =$ ☐
$3 \times 4 =$ ☐
$5 \times 6 =$ ☐
$2 \times 4 =$ ☐
$3 \times 5 =$ ☐
$5 \times 7 =$ ☐
$2 \times 5 =$ ☐
$3 \times 6 =$ ☐
$5 \times 8 =$ ☐
$2 \times 6 =$ ☐
$3 \times 7 =$ ☐
$5 \times 9 =$ ☐
$2 \times 7 =$ ☐
$3 \times 8 =$ ☐
$5 \times 4 =$ ☐
$2 \times 8 =$ ☐
$3 \times 9 =$ ☐
$2 \times 9 =$ ☐

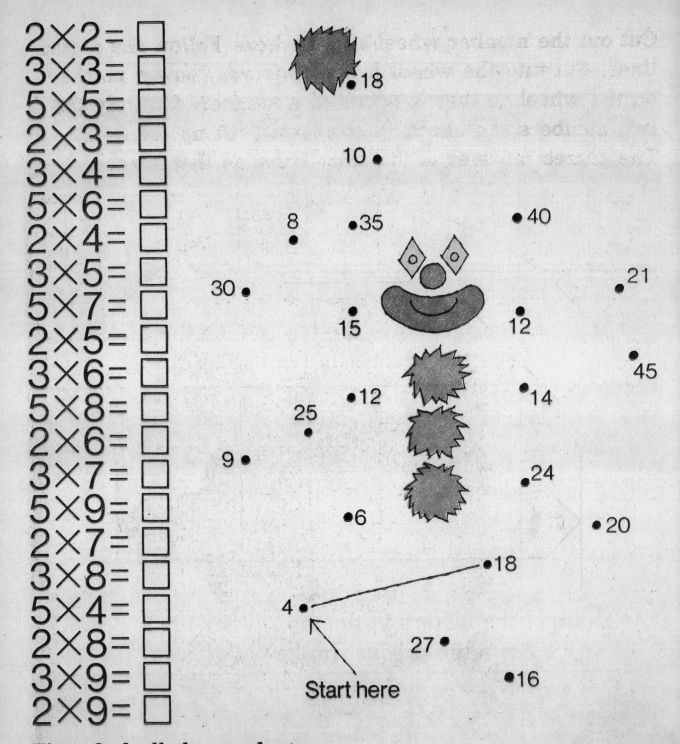

Start here

First find all the products.
Write the answers in the boxes.
Then connect the dots, starting with
the answer in the first box.

Cut out the number wheel and markers. Follow the dotted lines. Cut into the wheel to make doors. Place a marker on the wheel so that it points to a number. Multiply the two numbers. To check your answer, lift up the door. The correct answer is the same color as the marker.

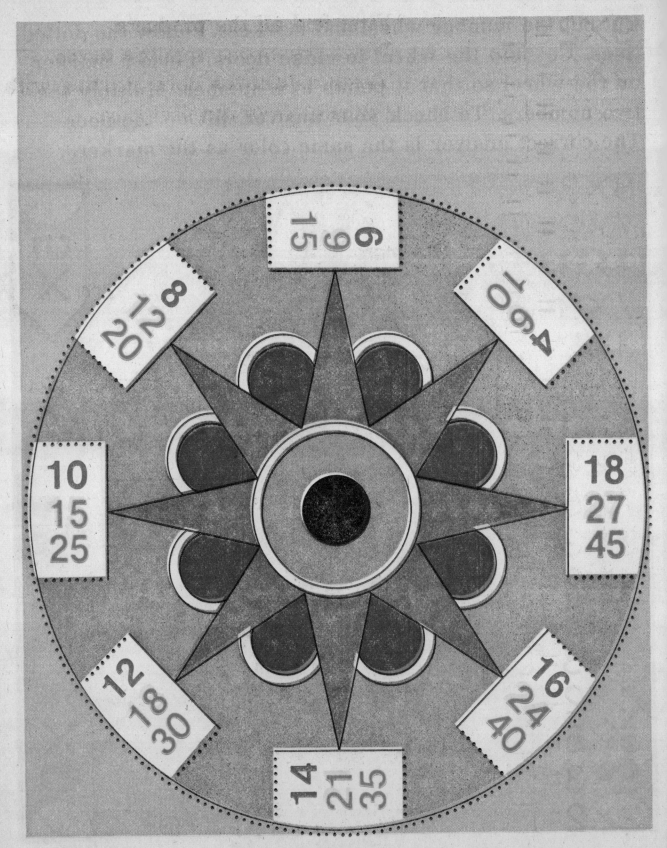

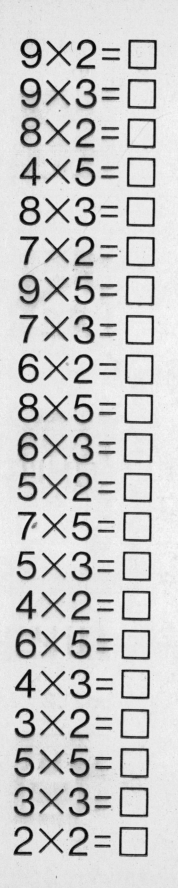

9×2=☐
9×3=☐
8×2=☐
4×5=☐
8×3=☐
7×2=☐
9×5=☐
7×3=☐
6×2=☐
8×5=☐
6×3=☐
5×2=☐
7×5=☐
5×3=☐
4×2=☐
6×5=☐
4×3=☐
3×2=☐
5×5=☐
3×3=☐
2×2=☐

**First find all the products.**
**Write the answers in the boxes.**
**Then connect the dots, starting with**
**the answer in the first box.**

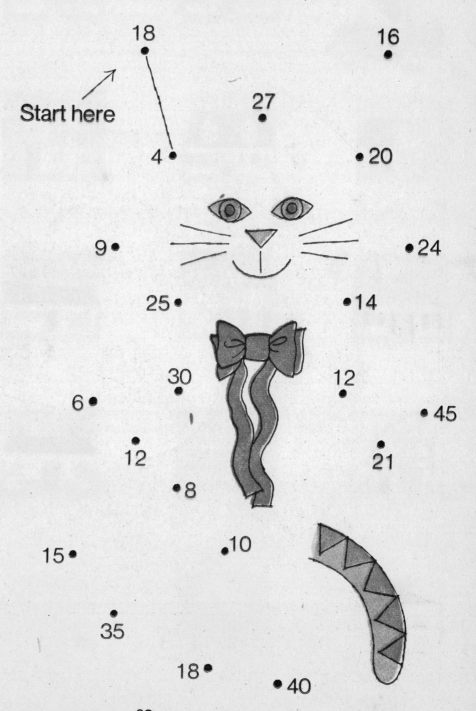

Start here

18   16
27
4   20
9   24
25   14
30   12
6   45
12   21
8
15   10
35
18   40

29

# Help Susie find her house. Count by 2's.
# Follow the signs that make the products from 2 to 20.

Start here

$2\times5=$     $2\times7=$

$2\times4=$     $2\times9=$

$2\times7=$     $2\times1=$     $2\times1=$

$2\times4=$     $2\times6=$     $2\times2=$     $2\times1=$

$2\times2=$     $2\times9=$     $2\times3=$

$2\times8=$     $2\times5=$     $2\times4=$     $2\times10=$

$2\times6=$     $2\times3=$     $2\times9=$

$2\times10=$     $2\times7=$     $2\times8=$     $2\times2=$

$2\times3=$     $2\times5=$     $2\times6=$

30

# One factor is 2. Color another numbered square to make the product in the pumpkin.

**18**

| 1 | 2 | 3 |
|---|---|---|
| 4 | 5 | 6 |
| 7 | 8 | 9 |

**10**

| 1 | 4 | 7 |
|---|---|---|
| 2 | 5 | 8 |
| 3 | 6 | 9 |

**16**

| 4 | 6 | 1 |
|---|---|---|
| 7 | 2 | 8 |
| 3 | 9 | 5 |

**8**

| 2 | 6 | 3 |
|---|---|---|
| 5 | 1 | 7 |
| 4 | 8 | 9 |

**14**

| 3 | 7 | 1 |
|---|---|---|
| 4 | 6 | 2 |
| 8 | 5 | 9 |

**6**

| 9 | 6 | 8 |
|---|---|---|
| 2 | 3 | 5 |
| 7 | 4 | 1 |

**12**

| 1 | 7 | 2 |
|---|---|---|
| 6 | 9 | 5 |
| 3 | 8 | 4 |

**4**

| 6 | 2 | 8 |
|---|---|---|
| 3 | 2 | 4 |
| 9 | 1 | 7 |

# Help the driver find his car. Count by 3's.
## Follow the signs that make the products from 3 to 30.

Start here →

3×9=

3×2=

3×3=

3×7=

3×4=

3×1=

3×5=

3×10=

3×8=

3×2=

3×6=

3×1=

3×6=

3×3=

3×2=

3×4=

3×8=

3×7=

3×9=

3×9=

3×4=

3×6=

3×10=

3×8=

3×5=

3×3=

3×1=

3×7=

3×5=

**One factor is 3. Color another numbered square to make the product in the apple.**

**27**

| 1 | 2 | 3 |
|---|---|---|
| 4 | 5 | 6 |
| 7 | 8 | 9 |

**24**

| 3 | 2 | 1 |
|---|---|---|
| 4 | 6 | 9 |
| 5 | 7 | 8 |

**21**

| 6 | 7 | 1 |
|---|---|---|
| 5 | 8 | 2 |
| 4 | 9 | 3 |

**18**

| 7 | 9 | 5 |
|---|---|---|
| 8 | 2 | 6 |
| 4 | 1 | 3 |

**15**

| 9 | 1 | 6 |
|---|---|---|
| 8 | 4 | 7 |
| 2 | 5 | 3 |

**12**

| 1 | 8 | 3 |
|---|---|---|
| 7 | 9 | 5 |
| 4 | 6 | 2 |

**9**

| 6 | 3 | 5 |
|---|---|---|
| 8 | 1 | 7 |
| 9 | 4 | 3 |

**6**

| 4 | 5 | 6 |
|---|---|---|
| 1 | 2 | 3 |
| 9 | 8 | 7 |

# Help the sailor find his boat. Count by 5's.
## Follow the signs that make the products from 5 to 50.

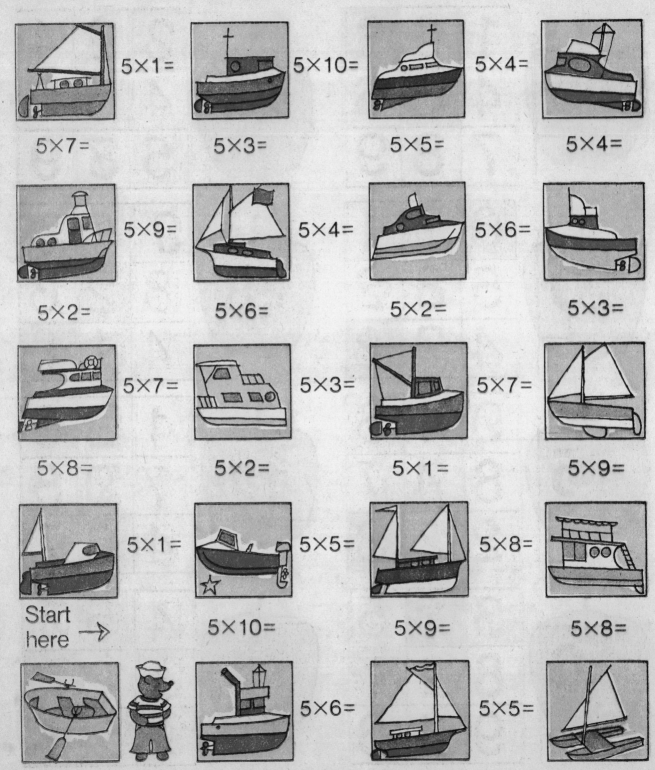

5×1=

5×10=

5×4=

5×4=

5×7=

5×3=

5×5=

5×4=

5×9=

5×4=

5×6=

5×2=

5×6=

5×2=

5×3=

5×7=

5×3=

5×7=

5×8=

5×2=

5×1=

5×9=

5×1=

5×5=

5×8=

Start here →

5×10=

5×9=

5×8=

5×6=

5×5=

# One factor is 5. Color another numbered square to make the product in the flag.

**45**

| 1 | 2 | 3 |
|---|---|---|
| 4 | 5 | 6 |
| 7 | 8 | 9 |

**25**

| 2 | 6 | 4 |
|---|---|---|
| 7 | 5 | 1 |
| 5 | 8 | 9 |

**40**

| 5 | 9 | 1 |
|---|---|---|
| 8 | 2 | 6 |
| 3 | 7 | 4 |

**20**

| 9 | 4 | 3 |
|---|---|---|
| 8 | 5 | 2 |
| 7 | 6 | 1 |

**35**

| 7 | 6 | 5 |
|---|---|---|
| 8 | 9 | 4 |
| 1 | 2 | 3 |

**15**

| 4 | 9 | 6 |
|---|---|---|
| 1 | 2 | 3 |
| 8 | 5 | 7 |

**30**

| 7 | 1 | 4 |
|---|---|---|
| 8 | 2 | 5 |
| 9 | 3 | 6 |

**10**

| 8 | 5 | 3 |
|---|---|---|
| 2 | 1 | 7 |
| 9 | 6 | 4 |

# Multiply the factors in the top row by the factor at the side. Write the product in the bottom box.

**4×**

| | 1 | 2 | 3 | 4 | 5 | 6 | 7 | 8 | 9 |
|---|---|---|---|---|---|---|---|---|---|
| | 4 | | | | | | | | |

**6×**

| | 1 | 2 | 3 | 4 | 5 | 6 | 7 | 8 | 9 |
|---|---|---|---|---|---|---|---|---|---|
| | 6 | | | | | | | | |

**7×**

| | 1 | 2 | 3 | 4 | 5 | 6 | 7 | 8 | 9 |
|---|---|---|---|---|---|---|---|---|---|
| | 7 | | | | | | | | |

**8×**

| | 1 | 2 | 3 | 4 | 5 | 6 | 7 | 8 | 9 |
|---|---|---|---|---|---|---|---|---|---|
| | 8 | | | | | | | | |

**9×**

| | 1 | 2 | 3 | 4 | 5 | 6 | 7 | 8 | 9 |
|---|---|---|---|---|---|---|---|---|---|
| | 9 | | | | | | | | |

# A Computer for Multiplication

To multiply 4 x 3, put your left finger on the blue 4.
That is one factor. Put your right finger on the red 3.
That is the other factor. Run your right finger down until
it is even with your left finger. The product is 12.
Now try   2 x 7,   3 x 6,   5 x 8,   8 x 7,   9 x 9.

| 1 | 2 | 3 | 4 | 5 | 6 | 7 | 8 | 9 |
|---|---|---|---|---|---|---|---|---|
| 2 | 4 | 6 | 8 | 10 | 12 | 14 | 16 | 18 |
| 3 | 6 | 9 | 12 | 15 | 18 | 21 | 24 | 27 |
| 4 | 8 | 12 | 16 | 20 | 24 | 28 | 32 | 36 |
| 5 | 10 | 15 | 20 | 25 | 30 | 35 | 40 | 45 |
| 6 | 12 | 18 | 24 | 30 | 36 | 42 | 48 | 54 |
| 7 | 14 | 21 | 28 | 35 | 42 | 49 | 56 | 63 |
| 8 | 16 | 24 | 32 | 40 | 48 | 56 | 64 | 72 |
| 9 | 18 | 27 | 36 | 45 | 54 | 63 | 72 | 81 |

| 1 | 2 | 3 | 4 | 5 | 6 | 7 | 8 | 9 |
|---|---|---|---|---|---|---|---|---|
| 2 | 4 | 6 | 8 | 10 | 12 | 14 | 16 | 18 |
| 3 | 6 | 9 | 12 | 15 | 18 | 21 | 24 | 27 |
| 4 | 8 | 12 | 16 | 20 | 24 | 28 | 32 | 36 |
| 5 | 10 | 15 | 20 | 25 | 30 | 35 | 40 | 45 |
| 6 | 12 | 18 | 24 | 30 | 36 | 42 | 48 | 54 |
| 7 | 14 | 21 | 28 | 35 | 42 | 49 | 56 | 63 |
| 8 | 16 | 24 | 32 | 40 | 48 | 56 | 64 | 72 |
| 9 | 18 | 27 | 36 | 45 | 54 | 63 | 72 | 81 |

$4 \times 4 = \square$    $6 \times 8 = \square$    $8 \times 7 = \square$

$4 \times 6 = \square$    $6 \times 9 = \square$    $8 \times 8 = \square$

$4 \times 7 = \square$    $7 \times 4 = \square$    $8 \times 9 = \square$

$4 \times 8 = \square$    $7 \times 6 = \square$    $9 \times 4 = \square$

$4 \times 9 = \square$    $7 \times 7 = \square$    $9 \times 6 = \square$

$6 \times 4 = \square$    $7 \times 8 = \square$    $9 \times 7 = \square$

$6 \times 6 = \square$    $7 \times 9 = \square$    $9 \times 8 = \square$

$6 \times 7 = \square$    $8 \times 4 = \square$    $9 \times 9 = \square$

$8 \times 6 = \square$

$4 \times 4 = \square$
$6 \times 6 = \square$
$7 \times 7 = \square$
$8 \times 8 = \square$
$9 \times 9 = \square$
$4 \times 6 = \square$
$6 \times 7 = \square$
$7 \times 8 = \square$
$8 \times 9 = \square$
$4 \times 7 = \square$
$6 \times 8 = \square$
$7 \times 9 = \square$
$4 \times 8 = \square$
$6 \times 9 = \square$
$4 \times 9 = \square$
$6 \times 4 = \square$
$7 \times 6 = \square$
$8 \times 7 = \square$
$9 \times 8 = \square$
$7 \times 4 = \square$
$8 \times 6 = \square$
$9 \times 4 = \square$
$8 \times 4 = \square$
$9 \times 6 = \square$
$9 \times 7 = \square$

**First find all the products.**
**Write the answers in the boxes.**
**Then connect the dots, starting with**
**the answer in the first box.**

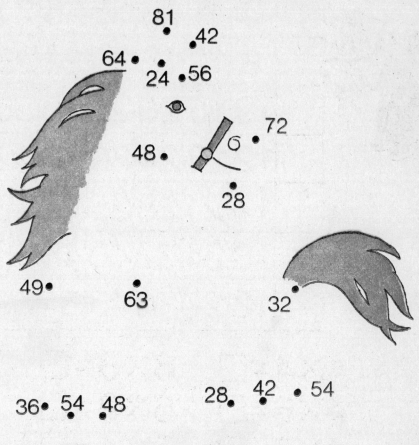

81
42
64
24  56
72
48
28
49
63
32
36  54  48
28  42  54

16
63
32  36
72  56
24  36

Start here

39

Count all the objects.
Write that number in the first box.
That is the <u>dividend</u>.

How many objects are in each set?
That number is in the middle box.
That is the <u>divisor</u>.

Count the number of sets.
Write that number in the last box.
That is the <u>quotient</u>, or missing factor.

<u>Division</u> is naming the missing factor.

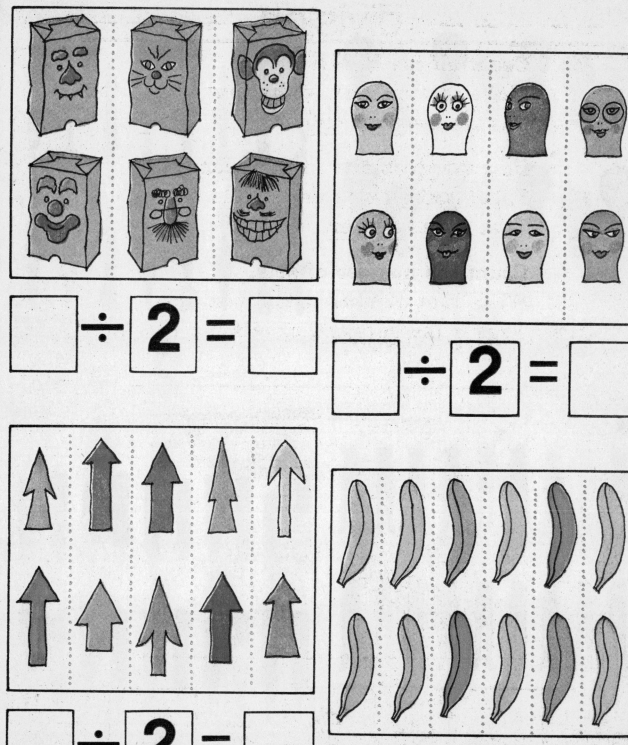

☐ ÷ **2** = ☐

☐ ÷ **2** = ☐

☐ ÷ **2** = ☐

☐ ÷ **2** = ☐

$\boxed{\phantom{00}} \div \boxed{2} = \boxed{\phantom{00}}$

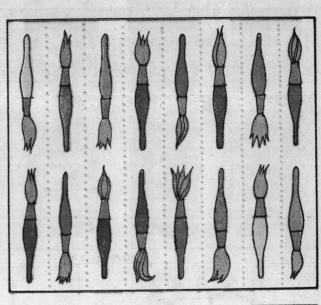

$\boxed{\phantom{00}} \div \boxed{2} = \boxed{\phantom{00}}$

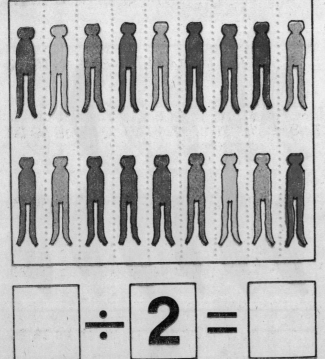

$\boxed{\phantom{00}} \div \boxed{2} = \boxed{\phantom{00}}$

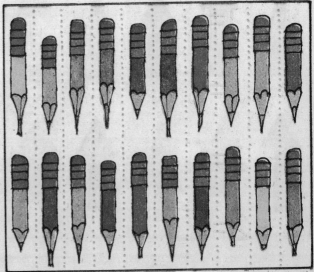

$\boxed{\phantom{00}} \div \boxed{2} = \boxed{\phantom{00}}$

**Starting from the dividend number,
jump to the left until you reach zero. Count your jumps.
That is the missing factor. You will see that dividing is a
short way of subtracting the same
number again and again.**

Start here

$4 \div 2 = \square$   0 1 2 3 4 5 6 7 8 9 10 11 12 13 14 15 16 17 18 19 20

$6 \div 2 = \square$   0 1 2 3 4 5 6 7 8 9 10 11 12 13 14 15 16 17 18 19 20

$8 \div 2 = \square$   0 1 2 3 4 5 6 7 8 9 10 11 12 13 14 15 16 17 18 19 20

$10 \div 2 = \square$   0 1 2 3 4 5 6 7 8 9 10 11 12 13 14 15 16 17 18 19 20

$12 \div 2 = \square$   0 1 2 3 4 5 6 7 8 9 10 11 12 13 14 15 16 17 18 19 20

$14 \div 2 = \square$   0 1 2 3 4 5 6 7 8 9 10 11 12 13 14 15 16 17 18 19 20

$16 \div 2 = \square$   0 1 2 3 4 5 6 7 8 9 10 11 12 13 14 15 16 17 18 19 20

$18 \div 2 = \square$   0 1 2 3 4 5 6 7 8 9 10 11 12 13 14 15 16 17 18 19 20

**Draw a line or lines to separate the objects into rows. The divisor tells you how many objects there should be in each row. Count the rows. Your answer is the missing factor.**

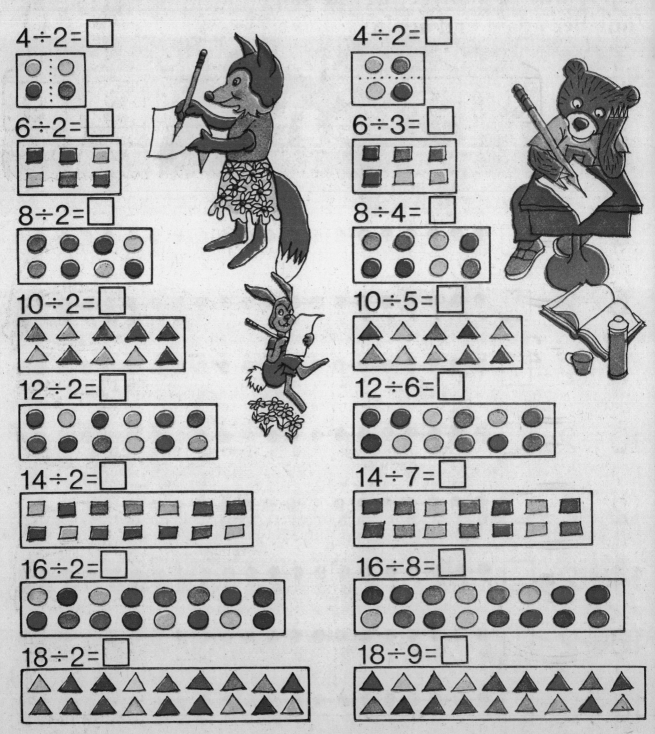

4÷2=□

6÷2=□

8÷2=□

10÷2=□

12÷2=□

14÷2=□

16÷2=□

18÷2=□

4÷2=□

6÷3=□

8÷4=□

10÷5=□

12÷6=□

14÷7=□

16÷8=□

18÷9=□

# Color the paint in each bucket the same
## color as the brush with the missing factor.

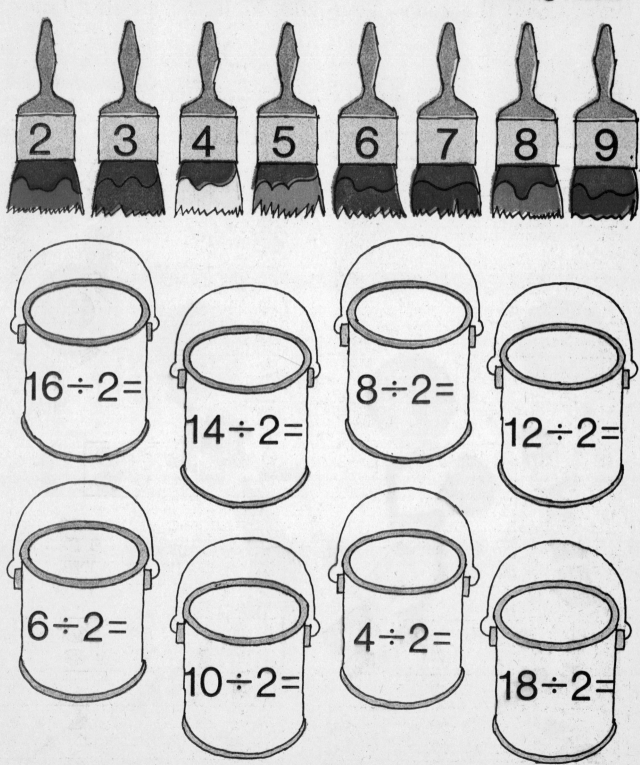

2  3  4  5  6  7  8  9

16 ÷ 2 =

14 ÷ 2 =

8 ÷ 2 =

12 ÷ 2 =

6 ÷ 2 =

10 ÷ 2 =

4 ÷ 2 =

18 ÷ 2 =

**Draw a line from each basketball to the basket with the missing factor.**

8

4

6

5

$8 \div 2 =$

$10 \div 2 =$

$12 \div 2 =$

$16 \div 2 =$

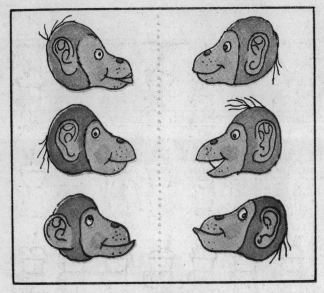

$6 \div 3 = 2$

$\boxed{\phantom{0}} \div \boxed{3} = \boxed{\phantom{0}}$

$\boxed{\phantom{0}} \div \boxed{3} = \boxed{\phantom{0}}$

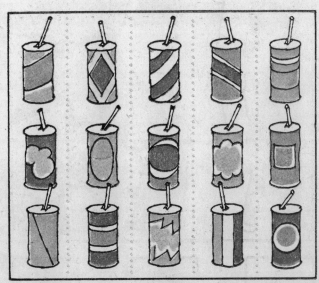

$\boxed{\phantom{0}} \div \boxed{3} = \boxed{\phantom{0}}$

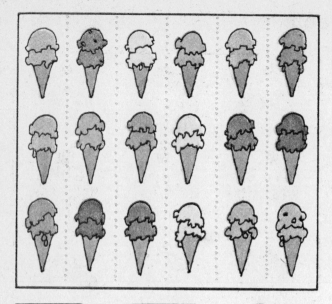

$$\boxed{\phantom{0}} \div \boxed{3} = \boxed{\phantom{0}}$$

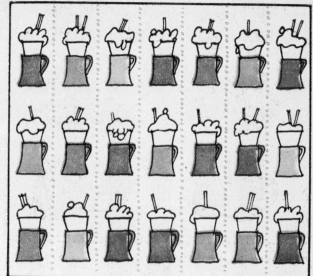

$$\boxed{\phantom{0}} \div \boxed{3} = \boxed{\phantom{0}}$$

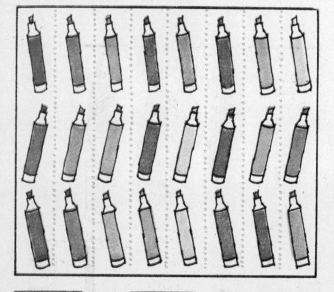

$$\boxed{\phantom{0}} \div \boxed{3} = \boxed{\phantom{0}}$$

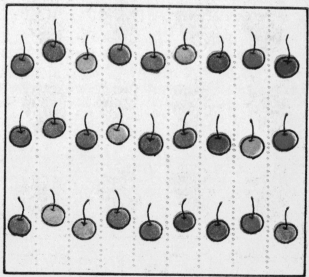

$$\boxed{\phantom{0}} \div \boxed{3} = \boxed{\phantom{0}}$$

**Starting from the dividend number,
jump to the left until you reach zero.
Count your jumps. That is the missing factor.**

Start here ↘

$6 \div 3 = \square$

0 1 2 3 4 5 6 7 8 9 10 11 12 13 14 15 16 17 18 19 20 21 22 23 24 25 26 27 28 29 30

$9 \div 3 = \square$

0 1 2 3 4 5 6 7 8 9 10 11 12 13 14 15 16 17 18 19 20 21 22 23 24 25 26 27 28 29 30

$12 \div 3 = \square$

0 1 2 3 4 5 6 7 8 9 10 11 12 13 14 15 16 17 18 19 20 21 22 23 24 25 26 27 28 29 30

$15 \div 3 = \square$

0 1 2 3 4 5 6 7 8 9 10 11 12 13 14 15 16 17 18 19 20 21 22 23 24 25 26 27 28 29 30

$18 \div 3 = \square$

0 1 2 3 4 5 6 7 8 9 10 11 12 13 14 15 16 17 18 19 20 21 22 23 24 25 26 27 28 29 30

$21 \div 3 = \square$

0 1 2 3 4 5 6 7 8 9 10 11 12 13 14 15 16 17 18 19 20 21 22 23 24 25 26 27 28 29 30

$24 \div 3 = \square$

0 1 2 3 4 5 6 7 8 9 10 11 12 13 14 15 16 17 18 19 20 21 22 23 24 25 26 27 28 29 30

$27 \div 3 = \square$

0 1 2 3 4 5 6 7 8 9 10 11 12 13 14 15 16 17 18 19 20 21 22 23 24 25 26 27 28 29 30

**Draw lines to separate the objects into rows. The divisor tells you how many objects there should be in each row. Count the rows. Your answer is the missing factor.**

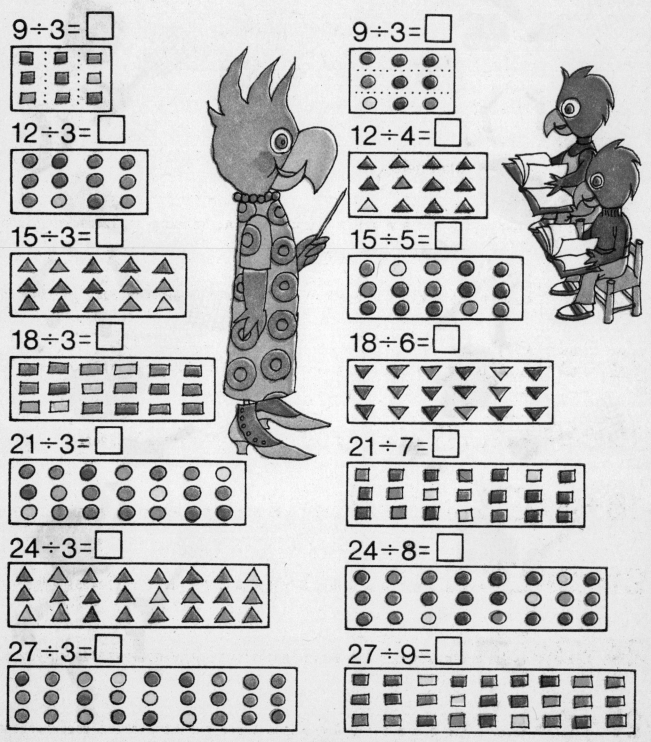

$9 \div 3 = \square$

$12 \div 3 = \square$

$15 \div 3 = \square$

$18 \div 3 = \square$

$21 \div 3 = \square$

$24 \div 3 = \square$

$27 \div 3 = \square$

$9 \div 3 = \square$

$12 \div 4 = \square$

$15 \div 5 = \square$

$18 \div 6 = \square$

$21 \div 7 = \square$

$24 \div 8 = \square$

$27 \div 9 = \square$

# Draw a line from each tennis player to
### the player with the missing factor.

52

# Color each purse the same color as the handkerchief with the missing factor.

$6 \div 3 =$

$9 \div 3 =$

$24 \div 3 =$

$15 \div 3 =$

$18 \div 3 =$

$21 \div 3 =$

$27 \div 3 =$

$12 \div 3 =$

2
3
4
5
6
7
8
9

$16 \div 4 = 4$      $\square \div 4 = \square$

$\square \div 5 = \square$      $\square \div 5 = \square$

**Starting from the dividend number, jump to the left until you reach zero. Count your jumps. That is the missing factor.**

Start here ↘

$16 \div 4 = \square$
0 1 2 3 4 5 6 7 8 9 10 11 12 13 14 15 16 17 18 19 20 21 22 23 24 25

$20 \div 2 = \square$
0 1 2 3 4 5 6 7 8 9 10 11 12 13 14 15 16 17 18 19 20 21 22 23 24 25

$20 \div 4 = \square$
0 1 2 3 4 5 6 7 8 9 10 11 12 13 14 15 16 17 18 19 20 21 22 23 24 25

$20 \div 5 = \square$
0 1 2 3 4 5 6 7 8 9 10 11 12 13 14 15 16 17 18 19 20 21 22 23 24 25

$25 \div 5 = \square$
0 1 2 3 4 5 6 7 8 9 10 11 12 13 14 15 16 17 18 19 20 21 22 23 24 25

Draw a line or lines to separate the objects into rows. The divisor tells you how many objects there should be in each row. Count the rows. Your answer is the missing factor.

$16 \div 4 = \square$

$16 \div 4 = \square$

$20 \div 2 = \square$

$20 \div 10 = \square$

$20 \div 4 = \square$

$20 \div 5 = \square$

$25 \div 5 = \square$

$25 \div 5 = \square$

Each child's shirt has a number.
Circle the child with the correct missing factor.

**There are two ways to write addition, subtraction, multiplication, and division problems:**

## ADDITION

$2+2=4$ or

$$\begin{array}{r} 2 \\ +2 \\ \hline 4 \end{array}$$

## SUBTRACTION

$4-2=2$ or

$$\begin{array}{r} 4 \\ -2 \\ \hline 2 \end{array}$$

## MULTIPLICATION

factor   factor  product
$2\times3=6$   or

$$\begin{array}{r} 3 \text{ factor} \\ \times 2 \text{ factor} \\ \hline 6 \text{ product} \end{array}$$

## DIVISION

dividend  divisor  missing factor or quotient
$6\div3=2$   or

divisor $3\overline{)6}$ missing factor or quotient / dividend

59

# Color each clown's hat to match the hat with the missing factor.

2 |4    4 |20    2 |8    2 |12    3 |24

2 |6    5 |25    2 |18    3 |27    3 |12

3 |21    4 |16    3 |6    5 |20    2 |10

2 |16    3 |15    2 |14    3 |9    3 |18

2    3    4    5    6    7    8    9

# A Computer for Division

To divide 12 by 3, put your left finger on the blue 3.
That is the divisor.

Put your right finger on the black 12 in the same row.
That is the dividend.

Run your right finger up to the top of that row to a red
number for the answer. The missing factor is 4.

Now try   4)20,   6)30,   7)21,   8)48.

| 1 | 2 | 3 | 4 | 5 | 6 | 7 | 8 | 9 |
|---|---|---|---|---|---|---|---|---|
| 2 | 4 | 6 | 8 | 10 | 12 | 14 | 16 | 18 |
| 3 | 6 | 9 | 12 | 15 | 18 | 21 | 24 | 27 |
| 4 | 8 | 12 | 16 | 20 | 24 | 28 | 32 | 36 |
| 5 | 10 | 15 | 20 | 25 | 30 | 35 | 40 | 45 |
| 6 | 12 | 18 | 24 | 30 | 36 | 42 | 48 | 54 |
| 7 | 14 | 21 | 28 | 35 | 42 | 49 | 56 | 63 |
| 8 | 16 | 24 | 32 | 40 | 48 | 56 | 64 | 72 |
| 9 | 18 | 27 | 36 | 45 | 54 | 63 | 72 | 81 |

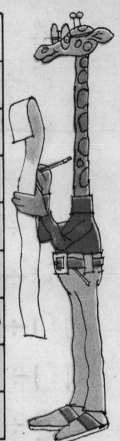

| 1 | 2 | 3 | 4 | 5 | 6 | 7 | 8 | 9 |
|---|---|---|---|---|---|---|---|---|
| 2 | 4 | 6 | 8 | 10 | 12 | 14 | 16 | 18 |
| 3 | 6 | 9 | 12 | 15 | 18 | 21 | 24 | 27 |
| 4 | 8 | 12 | 16 | 20 | 24 | 28 | 32 | 36 |
| 5 | 10 | 15 | 20 | 25 | 30 | 35 | 40 | 45 |
| 6 | 12 | 18 | 24 | 30 | 36 | 42 | 48 | 54 |
| 7 | 14 | 21 | 28 | 35 | 42 | 49 | 56 | 63 |
| 8 | 16 | 24 | 32 | 40 | 48 | 56 | 64 | 72 |
| 9 | 18 | 27 | 36 | 45 | 54 | 63 | 72 | 81 |

| | | | |
|---|---|---|---|
| 4⟌24 | 4⟌28 | 4⟌32 | 4⟌36 |
| 5⟌30 | 5⟌35 | 5⟌40 | 5⟌45 |
| 6⟌24 | 6⟌30 | 6⟌36 | 6⟌42 |
| 6⟌48 | 6⟌54 | 7⟌28 | 7⟌35 |
| 7⟌42 | 7⟌49 | 7⟌56 | 7⟌63 |
| 8⟌32 | 8⟌40 | 8⟌48 | 8⟌56 |
| 8⟌64 | 8⟌72 | 9⟌36 | 9⟌45 |
| 9⟌54 | 9⟌63 | 9⟌72 | 9⟌81 |

| | |
|---|---|
| $4 \div 2 = \square$ | $2 \times \square = 4$ |
| $6 \div 2 = \square$ | $3 \times \square = 6$ |
| $6 \div 3 = \square$ | $2 \times \square = 6$ |
| $8 \div 2 = \square$ | $4 \times \square = 8$ |
| $8 \div 4 = \square$ | $2 \times \square = 8$ |
| $9 \div 3 = \square$ | $3 \times \square = 9$ |
| $10 \div 2 = \square$ | $5 \times \square = 10$ |
| $10 \div 5 = \square$ | $2 \times \square = 10$ |
| $12 \div 2 = \square$ | $6 \times \square = 12$ |
| $12 \div 6 = \square$ | $2 \times \square = 12$ |
| $12 \div 3 = \square$ | $4 \times \square = 12$ |
| $12 \div 4 = \square$ | $3 \times \square = 12$ |
| $14 \div 2 = \square$ | $7 \times \square = 14$ |
| $14 \div 7 = \square$ | $2 \times \square = 14$ |
| $15 \div 3 = \square$ | $5 \times \square = 15$ |
| $15 \div 5 = \square$ | $3 \times \square = 15$ |
| $16 \div 2 = \square$ | $8 \times \square = 16$ |

| | |
|---|---|
| $16 \div 8 = \square$ | $2 \times \square = 16$ |
| $16 \div 4 = \square$ | $4 \times \square = 16$ |
| $18 \div 2 = \square$ | $9 \times \square = 18$ |
| $18 \div 9 = \square$ | $2 \times \square = 18$ |
| $18 \div 3 = \square$ | $6 \times \square = 18$ |
| $18 \div 6 = \square$ | $3 \times \square = 18$ |
| $20 \div 2 = \square$ | $10 \times \square = 20$ |
| $20 \div 10 = \square$ | $2 \times \square = 20$ |
| $20 \div 4 = \square$ | $5 \times \square = 20$ |
| $20 \div 5 = \square$ | $4 \times \square = 20$ |
| $21 \div 3 = \square$ | $7 \times \square = 21$ |
| $21 \div 7 = \square$ | $3 \times \square = 21$ |
| $24 \div 3 = \square$ | $8 \times \square = 24$ |
| $24 \div 8 = \square$ | $3 \times \square = 24$ |
| $25 \div 5 = \square$ | $5 \times \square = 25$ |
| $27 \div 3 = \square$ | $9 \times \square = 27$ |
| $27 \div 9 = \square$ | $3 \times \square = 27$ |